Nonsence Poems

Samuel Hill

BookLeaf Publishing

India | USA | UK

Presentation by *BookLeaf Publishing*

Web: www.bookleafpub.com

E-mail: info@bookleafpub.com

ISBN: 9789358736915

First edition 2023

To all who enjoy Fun and Wacky

ACKNOWLEDGEMENT

I'd like to thank the following people for listening and helping with my crazy and fun ideas;

Sarah Shelton, Daniel Riley, Tanya Goldsworthy, Kiley Starr, Hamish McArthur, Ernie Golubev and Ryan Starr.

Thank you to my parents for encourging me to write.

PREFACE

"Imagination is more important than knowledge. For knowledge is limited, whereas imagination embraces the entire world, stimulating progress, giving birth to evolution." - Albert Einstein

The Emu's Story

One day as I was walking
Along an autumn road
An emu popped in front of me
And had quite alot to say.

She told of the Blue Kangaroo
And the journey far he had to go
She spoke of the Green Koala
Sat high atop his lonely tree

She sang of the Pink Platypus
In the clouds they would swim
She said of the Purple Dingos
And the races they would hold

She asked if I heard tell
Of the Yellow Kookaburras
They laugh with pleasure
And weep with joy.

Yes, I've met them
They dance with the White Wombats
As they shine in the sunlight
They twinkle in the moonlight

She stated of the Red Echidna
Silent as the night
She remarked of mystery
The Orange Bilbies, rarely seen

Lastly she declared
Her own Black Emus
Who wandered alone
And told stories of their friends

The Dent Family

3

The dent family,
lived in a dent house.
The house was in a dent country,
In a dent world.

they were all alone on this small dent planet.

The Peter's Conundrum

Peter Pan had a van
Peter Pan had a can
In the van, he put the can
With the can, he put a fan

Peter Pen had a den
Peter Pen had a Ben
With the Ben, there was a Ken
With the men, there was a hen

Peter Pill was very ill
Peter Pill had a quill
Peter Pill had to kill
The ill he had
To enjoy his quill

Peter Pole had a mole
Peter Pole dug a hole
In the hole, he put the mole
To the mole, he gave some coal

Peter Pull had a bull
Peter Pull had some wool
With the wool he made a ball
To the bull, he gave the ball

Peter Pan knew Peter Pen
Peter Pen knew Peter Pill
Peter Pill knew Peter Pole
Peter Pole knew Peter Pull
Peter Pull knew Peter Pan

Yet

Peter Pull did not know Peter Pole
Peter Pole did not know Peter Pill
Peter Pill did not know Peter Pen
Peter Pen did not know Peter Pan
Peter Pan did not know Peter Pull

The Adventures of a Flea Named Floo

There once was a flea named Floo
Who lived in the South Australian zoo
He always went to work
With his brick and his berck
But he always came back
Because he was very slack

There Once was a flea named Floo
Who lived in the South Australian zoo
He was born and raised
By some very queer gays
He went to school
Where he met the lovely Ms. Moo

There once was a flea named Floo
Who lived in the South Australian zoo
He was a very musical person
But he always forgot his note
He already had a herson
But he never had a boat

There once was a flea named Floo
Who lived in the South Australian zoo
He took Ms. Moo on a date

To the fabulous zoo and its gate
There they got married
With their twelve dozen carried
And moved to an island
To the the beautiful shyland

There once was a flea named Floo
Who lived in the South Australian zoo
He lived till one hundred and four
But he died at one hundred and five
He had a fantastic life
With Ms. Moo as his wife
Then he went forevermore
To find the evermore

The Spider vs The Rain

8

The Spider was always told
Never go out in the rain

The Spider, he was so curious
Decided for once, he would

The Rain, it lashed so heavily
Upon his brittle legs

The Sun, finally came out
As did all the rest

And they found the Curious Spider
Dead upon the ground

Death comes a'knocking

As I was working, one day
Death came a'knocking
He asked for a cup of sugar
And then went on his way

A week went by, I was in my garden
Death came a'knocking
He asked for a pint of milk
And took it to his house

'Twas in the middle of writing, about three
months ago
Death came a'knocking
He asked for eight dozen eggs, laid yesterday
morning
Don't ask me how he carried them, all the way
back home

There I was, spring cleaning
Death came a'knocking
He asked for a bowl of fruit
Then walked to his abode

Reading a favourite book of mine
Death came a'knocking

he asked for a sunflower seed
Then sauntered to his dwelling

Coming home from a walk
Death came a'knocking
He asked for a ton of apples
He dashed to his refuge

And finally, last night around 2
Death came a'knocking
He asked for a kind soul, whose time it was to
leave
I left my body willingly, still tucked up in bed
Left my home peacefully, and followed him into
the night

Tiger Time

Tiger Time was an old soul
He'd seen many things,
And done alot too.
He'd seen trees born, grow and die,
And the rivers dry up.
He'd seen the dinosaurs roam,
And the meteor that struck
He'd helped the cavemen with fire
And marvelled at the wheel
He'd seen the last dodo,
Wiped from the earth.

Walking in the Woods

12

Walking in the woods
It's quite a peaceful scene
Birds are singing delicious melodies
Bees gathering sweet nectar
Flowers are blooming brightly
Wind whistling through the trees
Soft grass beneath your bare feet
Warmth of the sun in the air

The Fallen King

The King of Dragons
He heard of a village
Such an awful village
Full of wicked men
Who killed dragons
For a sport

Yet not such an awful village
The stories, greatly exaggerated
Only a rather small group
Would go out to hunt
To slaughter innocent dragons

The King, he would not listen
He flew to the village
So full of hate
He did not see

The fire and the smoke
It choked everyone
And snuffed it all out

He returned, so full of pride
The Queen saw only a Monster

A Fallen King

Now he sits
Atop the clock

Blackened tower
Forever broken
Full of sorrow

Clock tower now stands
The middle of a ruin
Every other structure
Burned down to a crisp

The King
He misses his home
Yet he will not return
Others come to see
Hear a woeful tale

His misdeeds now forgotten
By all, except The Queen
Never will she forgive
Those who kill willingly
For no other gain
Then to get their revenge

A Cat's Tail

My name is Charles von Fluffybuns
I've traveled across the land
I've braved the depths of the ocean
And explored the wide open space

The giant Blubbering Mongles
Their tears make the rain
Only the tiny Rayhogs
Can cease the torrent of misery

The mystery, deep beneath the sea
Is only a small blind bone
It came from an ancient jewel
Named the shattering misty shardense

O the planet of the Twine
Where the sugarberries grow
They twist and turn often
To keep them cold and warm

I searched the skies above
Fore the Batty Ratty Birds
Who fly to the Isle of Life
In search of their short found songs

In the Darkness of the Depths
There lives a lonely Octimun
She was the last of her kind
The first orange seed

The void beyond the sheet
A group of star shined Fingles
The inventors of nothing
Will end all of humour

Far off country lane
I almost missed entirely
The trees are made of flesh
Their leaves taste sour and swift

Ghosts live on forever
Mine are all but gone
I hoped you enjoyed my journey
As king of the just and proud

Vanilla; The Coke

17

The coke fizzed sweetly
The vanilla was so strong
The taste was just great

Scrabble

Rough is Dry
Nine will Join
Tulips Sway
The Bold are Toed
Films of Bikes
You can't have a Zag
Without a Zig
Quiet went the Glue
A Taxi needs a Tire
Raisins have no Pine
The feast of Drones
Jade must Heel
Facts Age
Glory to the Zany
My Fate is Windy
Have a Daisy Bath
Truer Quids were never found
Ding goes the Ping
A Haunted Jar
The Key to the Tokens

A Night to Remember

A night in Lego
Vampire by night
Asleep by day
He went to the club
To dance his sorrows away

A young Warlock
Only a few centuries old
Born in the bay
He flew to the club
To skip his troubles away

In the middle
These two, do meet
Sparks seem to fly
As they grow closer
Both an attractive guy

Blocks all around
But no one sees
This wonderful bliss
They draw near
To share a secret kiss

The Wrong Grapes

Small orbs, so round
They come from the ground
Green as can be
Like words from a tree
They weigh less than a pound

Lightning Strike

21

I was struck on the head
Thought I'd be dead
Now I'm baking bread

Pebbles Unite

Soft and smooth, they grow
Washed before the sea
We give a sense of woe
Feet step, we gain some glee

Dancing on the frog's head
To laugh and shout with mirth
Eventually we go to bed
Inside the deep dark earth

Midnight Express

Us ghosts are wild and free
We live beneath the trees
We come out in the night
To dance to our delight

The train comes to collect
Before we can get swept
To take us into town
Where we can find our crown

Once more inside the carriage
We float in single file
A witness to their marriage
It ends with a smile

The Midnight Express
Will stop at every shadow
In order to impress
The late night endless sorrow

At last we make it home
To rest before we roam
We do not like to fight
Instead we must give flight

Charm of a Chair

Here I stand in the shop
Waiting to be bought
I was made with greatest care
Out of the finest wood

I have swirls upon my arms
And curves in my feet
My head is an art piece
Full of character and charm

It ripples like water
So elegant and sweet
My lap is of silk
Like a cat's sleek coat

My back is tall
My legs are short
Yet I stand here with grace
Under my personal spot light

I'm ash in wood
Chestnut in colour
My appearance is old
But my age is young

I'm strong in most ways
But fragile in others
When you buy me, take care
As I'm expensive and unique

Nutty Haikus

Brothers on my right
My sisters on my left
 Ten family trees

The moon shines brightly
 Upon the sleepy planet
 Everyone is gone

 A celebration
Party size does not matter
 Strawberry filled cake

 Dancing aliens
Are full of mischief and spite
 Making the suns fight

The Ways of a Weed

Oxalis is a family
Just like you and me
While most are sweet and pretty
One is just a weed

This poor little weed
So sour and yellow
She lives all alone
Unable to be mellow

But is she a weed
Or a misunderstood flower
Her heart full of gold
Locked in a tower

Will she ever be freed
To grow like her sisters
Admired and loved
For her beautiful whiskers

There's no happy ending
For this wild sad flower
Unless we change our minds
About weeds and their power

Mayhem & Macabre

Mayhem and his partner Macabre
Were a pair that people thought quite bizarre
With chaos they'd flirt
In the night, they'd assert
Their dark reign leaving towns in a scar

Mayhem and Macabre, lovers entwined
In the shadows of night, their hearts aligned
With passion and fire
Their love did inspire
A bond so deep, in darkness designed

Mayhem and Macabre, Their love so strong
Decided to marry, where they belong
In a ceremony unique and rare
With darkness and chaos in the air
Their union was celebrated all night long

www.ingramcontent.com/pod-product-compliance
Lightning Source LLC
La Vergne TN
LVHW051244200726

843510LV00011B/1676